WILDLIFE AT RISK

ELEPHANTS

Ian Redmond

The Bookwright Press
New York • 1990

Wildlife at Risk

Bears   Elephants
Birds of Prey   Tigers

Cover: An African elephant, ready to charge if attacked.

First published in the
United States in 1990 by
The Bookwright Press
387 Park Avenue South
New York, NY 10016

First published in 1990 by
Wayland (Publishers) Ltd
61 Western Road, Hove
East Sussex, BN3 1JD, England

Library of Congress Cataloging-in-Publication Data

Redmond, Ian.
    Elephants/by Ian Redmond.
      p. cm. – (Wildlife at risk)
    Includes bibliographical references.
    Summary: Discusses the physical characteristics, habitat,
behavior, and endangered nature of the elephant.
    ISBN 0–531–18354–8
    1. Elephants – Juvenile literature. [1. Elephants. 2. Rare
animals. 3. Wildlife conservation.] I. Title. II. Series.
QL737.P98R63   1990
599.6′1 – dc20   90–446
                                   CIP
                                   AC

Typeset by Nicola Taylor, Wayland
Printed in Italy by L.E.G.O. S.p.A., Vicenza

Contents

Words printed in **bold** are explained in
the glossary on page 30.

THE GENTLE GIANTS

Elephants are the largest animals living on land today. There are two different **species** of elephants, the African elephant and the Asian elephant. Asian elephants are sometimes called Indian elephants, but they live in many other Asian countries as well as India.

African elephants have very large ears. They are shaped roughly like the map of Africa. Asian elephants have smaller ears that are shaped roughly like the map of India. Both male and female African elephants have **tusks**. Female Asian elephants do not have tusks.

Female elephants are called cows. Male elephants are called bulls. Baby elephants are called calves.

*Both African elephants (**left**) and Asian elephants (**right**) spend much of their time feeding. Can you spot the main differences between the two species? Use the diagram on the opposite page to help you.*

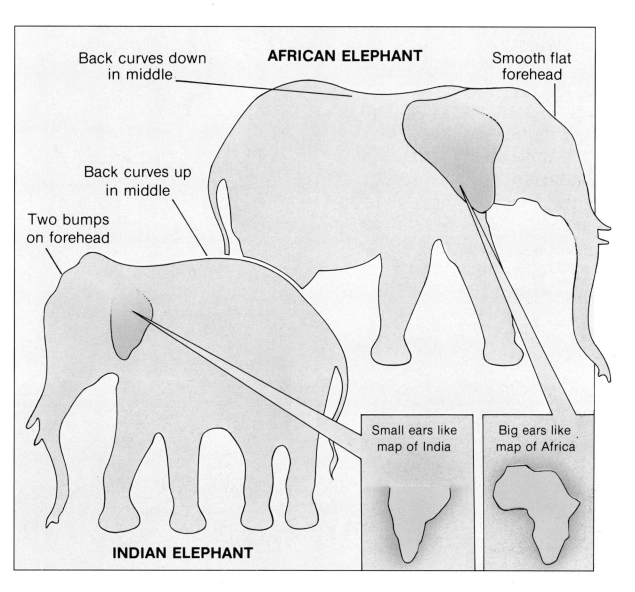

Back curves down in middle

AFRICAN ELEPHANT

Smooth flat forehead

Back curves up in middle

Two bumps on forehead

Small ears like map of India

Big ears like map of Africa

INDIAN ELEPHANT

The elephant has legs that are built like pillars, to support the weight of its huge body. When an elephant is standing, the bones inside its legs are stacked on top of each other. All its weight is resting on the tips of its toes. With such long legs, an elephant cannot lower its massive head to the ground to eat grass, like a horse. Instead, it feeds itself with its nose!

The elephant's nose and upper lip have grown together to form a trunk. In prehistoric times, many kinds of animals had trunks, including the **mammoths** and the **mastodons**. Today, the elephant is the only animal that has a trunk. The African elephant has heavy folds of skin on its trunk, and it has two "fingers" at the tip. The Asian elephant's trunk is smoother and it has only one "finger" at the tip.

Above An African elephant gathering grass with its trunk.

Left An African elephant can pick leaves and nuts with the "fingers" at the tip of its trunk.

The elephant can use its powerful bendy trunk in the same way people use their arms. It can coil its trunk around a massive log to lift it, or it can pick a single leaf from a tree, using the finger-like tip of the trunk.

When an elephant is old enough to feed itself, it puts everything it eats into its mouth using its trunk. A baby elephant, however, has no idea what to do with the funny rubbery trunk that squirms around on the front of its face. To drink milk from its mother's breast, it flops its trunk onto its forehead and drinks with its mouth.

An elephant calf sucking milk from its mother. Calves feed on milk until they are about two years old.

WHERE ELEPHANTS LIVE

Elephants are able to live in many different **habitats**. Some live in rocky deserts, others live in **rainforests**. Some live very high in the mountains. They can climb steep slopes and walk along narrow mountain paths. The skin on their feet is very tough and wrinkled, like a car tire. This helps them to grip the ground as they walk. But if a slope is too steep for them to climb down easily, they sit back and slide down on their bottoms!

Asian elephants like to live in forests. Some African elephants like to live in forests too. They are called forest elephants. Other elephants live on the open plains of Africa. This area is called the **savannah**. The elephants that live there are called savannah elephants.

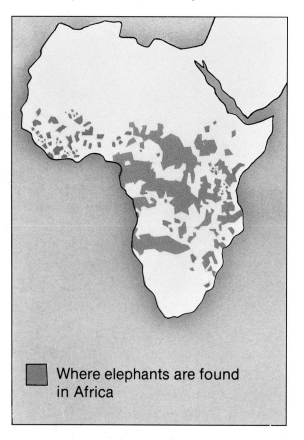

Where elephants are found in Africa

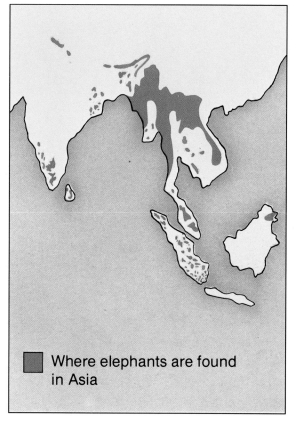

Where elephants are found in Asia

Like African elephants, Asian elephants live in areas where there is forest, grassland and plenty of water.

African elephants wandering over the open plains of the savannah.

Elephants eat hundreds of different kinds of plants. They need to live where they can find many different kinds of food. The best places have patches of forest mixed with savannah. When the grass on the savannah is dry and yellow, the elephants can move into the shade of the trees. When the rains come, they can move out to feed on the savannah again.

LIFE WITH THE HERD

Young elephants learn from the older members of the family herd where to find food and water. They also learn where to dig for salt, as this picture shows.

Like humans, elephants live in family groups. Their family groups are called herds. The family is led by an old female elephant. She is called the matriarch. Some elephants live for a very long time – about sixty years.

Baby elephants are looked after very carefully by their mothers. The cow elephants in a family herd usually help one another to look after the calves. Some mothers allow calves that are not their own to suck milk from them.

Big babies

- The baby elephant develops inside its mother for almost two years before it is ready to be born. No other animal develops for such a long time inside its mother.

- Elephants weigh about 220 pounds (100 kg) when they are born.

- A female elephant usually has one calf every four or five years.

- Elephant mothers produce a watery milk from breasts between their front legs. Newborn elephants have to stretch up to reach the nipples. When they are one year old, they are just short enough to walk under the mother's chest.

Swamps are good places for feeding and wallowing – but this calf is struggling to keep up with its mother.

The calves have to learn many things as they grow up. They must learn where to find food and water and how to live in a family group. Bull and cow elephants begin to play in different ways. The cows find out how to care for babies by looking after their younger brothers and sisters. Bulls spend more time play-fighting with their friends.

They push and shove each other, clash tusks and wrestle with their trunks. This helps their muscles to develop. They will need to know how to fight when they are older. Play-fighting also helps them to find out how strong they are compared with other young bulls in the area. The weaker males give way to the strongest bull.

A family of elephants enjoying a mud-bath. The mud helps the elephants to keep cool.

Young cow elephants learn how to be good mothers by helping to look after the calves in their family herd.

When they are about fourteen years old, the bull elephants leave their family herd, or are thrown out of it. They live on their own or with other bulls. They visit the cow elephants only to breed. A bull might not **mate** until he is thirty years old, but a cow has usually had her first calf by the time she is fifteen.

Young bulls clash tusks and wrestle with their trunks.

WORKING ELEPHANTS

Elephants are very strong, so people use these animals to help them in their work. Thousands of years ago African elephants were used in battles. They were like living tanks and they terrified the enemy armies.

Asian elephants have also been used for thousands of years. In Burma, elephants were used to drag logs out of the steep valleys where the trees grew. There was no other way of getting the logs out. In the 1930s, more than 6,000 elephants were being used for this job in Burma.

An Asian elephant at work in northern Thailand.

Left *African elephants can be trained too. The first elephant to be called "Jumbo" was a bull African elephant. He was kept at London Zoo between 1865 and 1882 and gave rides to visitors.*

The elephants are not specially bred to be used for work. When a wild elephant is captured, it soon becomes tame enough to be trained. Cow elephants are easier to train than bull elephants.

Wild bull elephants used to mate with trained cow elephants when the cow elephants were left to feed in the forests at night. Now there are so few wild Asian elephants that this hardly ever happens. Scientists are trying to find ways of collecting **sperm** from bull elephants and putting it into the **wombs** of cow elephants, so that more of the trained elephants will be able to have babies.

Decorated elephants are on sale here at this elephant market in northern India.

ELEPHANTS IN DANGER

Elephants once lived in many parts of Africa and southern Asia. They had an important effect on their surroundings. When there was no rain for a long time, elephants dug for water with their tusks. They pushed over small trees to feed on nuts and leaves. They even helped to make new forests grow, because they passed tree seeds in their droppings. This made their habitat better for them to live in, and better for the other animals that lived there too, including humans.

Above *Elephants dig in earth to find salt to eat.*

As people take more land to build homes, the elephant's habitats are destroyed.

Today, the areas where elephants live have become much fewer. In many places, their habitat is being destroyed. The elephants need trees and grass for food, but humans also need land so they can grow crops. As the number of humans grows, more land is needed to grow crops. Humans take over the land that the elephants used to live on.

Elephants love to play in water. Sometimes they go under water and use their trunks as snorkels.

What an elephant needs

- **Food** – elephants eat 330-500 pounds (150-225 kg) of fresh greens, roots, bark, buds and fruit each day.

- **Water** – an adult elephant drinks more than 53 gallons (200 l) per day, and likes to bathe to keep cool and moist.

- **Mud** – elephants plaster on mud to prevent sunburn and bites from flies.

- **Salt** – elephants need salt to live. They cannot lick salt from rocks, so they use their tusks to break off lumps of salt rock to eat.

- **Space** – an elephant may need as much as 1,000 square miles (2,500 sq km) of land.

No one knows exactly how many elephants there are in the world. Scientists need to find out how many there are, so that they can work out the best way to protect elephants. Elephants that live on the savannah can usually be seen from an airplane. It is quite easy to count them. But they stand in the shade of trees during the hottest part of the day, trying to keep cool. Then they cannot be seen from an airplane. They are hidden by the trees.

Elephants standing under a tree in the savannah. They are trying to find shelter from the midday sun.

Rangers figure out how many elephants live in an area by counting piles of dung.

Elephants living in forests cannot be counted from an airplane at all. Cars and trucks cannot be driven through the thick forest, so the only way to count the elephants is on foot.

Counting elephants in this way sounds like very dangerous work. Sometimes the trees and bushes are so thick that you can see only a little way ahead. You never know whether a large animal is going to be around the next bend in the path. But the people counting the elephants do not try to find and count every herd. Instead, they walk in a straight line through the forest and count all the piles of dung that they see. Then they can estimate how many elephants are living nearby.

There are four forest elephants in this picture. Can you see them all?

Although it is very difficult to count living elephants, we can figure out how many elephants have been killed. Many elephants are killed every year because people want the **ivory** that their tusks are made from. By counting the number of tusks that have been sold, scientists can figure out how many elephants have been killed.

Left Even female elephants, with their slender tusks, are killed by ivory poachers.

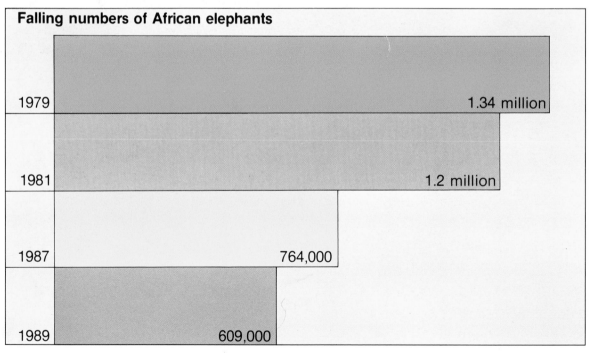

Falling numbers of African elephants

1979	1.34 million
1981	1.2 million
1987	764,000
1989	609,000

An elephant's jaw-bone. In many parts of Africa, there are more dead elephants than living ones.

In some places, there may be too many elephants living in a small area. This usually happens because elephants have come to live in a **national park** or **reserve**, where they are protected by the **rangers**. In most parts of Africa, elephant numbers have fallen very quickly. They are remaining at the same level, or growing, only in South Africa, Zimbabwe, Botswana, Malawi and Namibia. If the number of elephants continues to fall as quickly as it did in the early 1980s, the African elephant will become **extinct** in the wild in less than twenty years.

IVORY POACHING

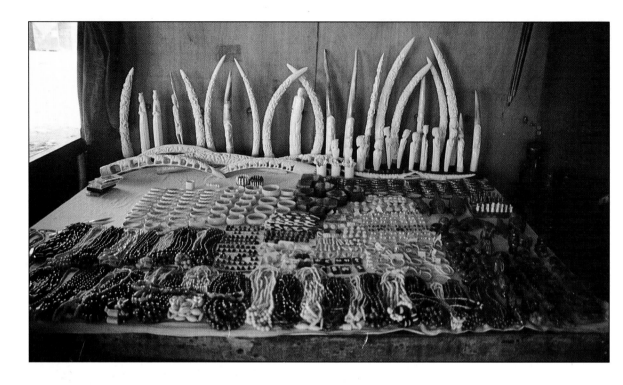

At least seventeen elephants must have been killed to make the jewelry and carvings on sale here.

An elephant's tusks are made of ivory. Ivory was used to make many different things before plastics were invented. Piano keys, hairbrushes, chess pieces and jewelry were all made from ivory. Nowadays, all these things can be made from other materials.

Ivory is still used to make carvings and jewelry. In some African countries, people are allowed to kill a certain number of elephants, so that they can use the tusks to make these ivory ornaments. But every year, people kill more elephants than they are allowed, in order to steal the tusks. This is called poaching. Ivory is very expensive. The **poachers** can get a lot of money for the ivory that they have stolen.

Tusk facts

- The record length for a tusk is 11.32 ft (3.45 m) and the record weight for a single tusk is 258 pounds (117 kg).

- Tusks grow about 6.7 inches (17 cm) each year. The tusk is made of dentine, or ivory. Only elephant ivory has diamond-shaped, criss-crossed lines running through it.

- Elephants have small "milk **tushes**" when they are born. When they are about one year old, the tushes are replaced by permanent tusks. The tusks cannot be seen until the elephant is about two and a half years old.

In Zimbabwe, some elephants have to be killed because there are too many living in a small area. This is called culling.

In Africa, many elephants are shot by gangs of people, who will murder anyone who tries to stop them. This even happens in wildlife parks. The gangs often have better guns and equipment than the park rangers. The poachers kill whole herds with their machine guns. Then they hack out the tusks and escape into the bush before the park rangers arrive.

Below *Rangers weigh ivory taken from poachers.*

Below *A bull elephant, killed for a few pounds of ivory.*

Orphaned elephants and rhinos are cared for at Daphne Sheldrick's Animal Orphanage in Kenya.

Not all poachers belong to organized gangs. Some poachers kill elephants living near them, using very cruel methods. Wire traps are used to trap elephants around the trunk, so that they cannot feed. Their water holes are poisoned. Spikes are set in the paths where elephants walk, to cut their feet and legs. The elephants die slowly and painfully – but the poachers are thinking only about the money that they will get for the ivory.

Poachers used to kill mainly bull elephants with large tusks. But now most of the elephants with large, heavy tusks have been killed. This means that for every ton of ivory they get, the poachers have to kill more elephants. Even small calves without tusks die because their mothers have been killed by poachers.

FIGHTING THE POACHERS

The rangers have to use as many ways as possible to try to catch the poachers. Sometimes the warden flies overhead in a small airplane. When he sees something suspicious, he uses his radio to tell his men on the ground and they will then begin to search the area.

If they do not have an airplane, the rangers rely on people called trackers. If poachers enter a park or reserve, trackers follow their trail until they catch up with the poachers. This often happens at night, when the poachers settle down to make a campfire. The trackers lead the rangers to the camp. Then the rangers rush in and arrest the poachers. It is dangerous work.

Park rangers need trucks, radios and better guns to help them in their fight against the poachers.

People showing their support for a ban on the ivory trade.

If the poachers see the rangers, they often shoot at them. Both the rangers and the poachers are sometimes killed. Poachers who are found guilty may be put in prison for several years.

There is another way to fight the poachers. Poachers only kill elephants because they will be paid a lot of money when they sell the ivory. But most governments now refuse to let ivory be brought into their countries. This makes it harder for the poachers to sell the ivory. When the poachers can no longer sell ivory at all, there will be no point in stealing it. Then the killing of elephants for their tusks may stop.

THE FUTURE FOR ELEPHANTS

An Asian elephant enjoying a shower. African and Asian elephants are now on the list of endangered species.

In 1989, **conservationists** from 103 countries met to decide on the best ways to protect the African elephant and control the ivory trade. They decided that the African elephant should have the same protection as the Asian elephant. People are no longer allowed to send ivory from Africa to be sold in other countries. But ivory poaching may continue, because some countries do not agree that the ivory trade should be banned. The ivory trade will stop only when people refuse to buy ivory. If you see ivory carvings or jewelry for sale, remember that an elephant has probably been killed to make them.

Many schoolchildren in African countries join clubs to find out more about wildlife. The clubs are based on the Wildlife Clubs of Kenya, which were set up more than twenty years ago. The children go to talks, films and slide shows about wildlife. Sometimes, they go on a field trip into a national park or reserve to watch the animals.

Many of the people who now work in Kenya's national parks were in the Wildlife Club when they were at school. They are interested in wildlife and are working to protect the animals and their habitats. With the help of people like these, there may be a better future for elephants, and all wildlife, throughout Asia and Africa.

The future of Africa's elephants, and of all the world's wildlife, lies in our hands.

Glossary

Conservationists People who work to protect animals and plants.

Extinct When the last member of a particular species has died, it is said to be extinct. The dinosaurs are extinct, for example.

Habitats The natural homes or surroundings of any plant or animal.

Ivory The material from which elephant's tusks are made.

Mammoths Large, hairy, elephant-like animals with long curved tusks. Mammoths lived in prehistoric times.

Mastodons Animals that looked like mammoths but were smaller.

Mate To pair as male and female to produce babies.

National park An area of land controlled and protected by the government where animals can live more safely.

Poachers People who break the law by killing animals.

Rainforest Thick forest that grows in tropical areas where there is heavy rainfall.

Rangers People who work in a national park or reserve and protect its wildlife.

Reserve An area of land where wildlife is protected.

Savannah Open grassland with only a few bushes or trees.

Species Any kind of animal or plant that can breed to produce more of the same kind.

Sperm The cells produced by a male that join with a female's egg, or ovum, to produce a baby.

Tushes Small tusks that stick out only a little way.

Tusks The long front teeth of an elephant that grow out of the front of the face.

Womb The part of a female's body where a baby develops before it is born.

Further reading

If you would like to find out more about elephants, you might like to read some of the following books.

Elephants by Norman S. Barrett (Franklin Watts, 1988).
Endangered Animals by Dean Morris (Raintree Publishers, 1984).

Endangered Animals by Lynn M. Stone (Children's Press, 1982).

Useful addresses

If you would like to get involved in the conservation of elephants and other rare animals throughout the world, you might like to contact one of the organizations listed below.

Audubon Naturalist Society of the Central Atlantic States
8940 Jones Mill Road
Chevy Chase, Maryland 20815
301–652–9188

The Conservation Foundation
1717 Massachusetts Avenue, N.W.
Washington D.C. 20036
202–797–4300

Elephant Interest Group
106 East Hickory Grove Road
Bloomfield Hills
Michigan 48013

The Humane Society of the USA
2100 L Street, N.W.
Washington D.C. 20037
202–452–1100

The International Fund for Animal Welfare
P.O. Box 193
Yarmouth Port, Massachusetts 02675
617–363–4944

National Wildlife Federation
1412 16th Street, N.W.
Washington D.C. 20036
202–797–6800

Index

Picture acknowledgments

The photographs in this book were supplied by Oxford Scientific Films from the following photographers: Anthony Bannister 6 (top), 12; G.I. Bernard 21; Mike Birkhead 23; Stanley Breeden 9 (top), 28; David Cayless 7, 11, 25; Waina Cheng 4 (right);Carol Farneti 17; Richard Packwood 13, 18, 29; Ian Redmond 4 (left), 9 (bottom), 14 (bottom), 16 (bottom), 19 (top, bottom), 20, 22, 24 (top, bottom) 27; Edwin Sadd cover, 10, 16 (top); Frank Schneidermeyer 13; Dr. Nigel Smith 14 (top); Belinda Wright 15. All artwork is by John Yates.